Stop Being Invisible
Workbook

By Dion McIntosh

A DIY Branding Product

for Bad People Books I Los Angeles

Stop Being Invisible
Workbook

This workbook is best used along with the book
Stop Being Invisible: Start Building A Human Brand Of Greater Influence.

By Dion McIntosh

First Edition

Cover & layout design by Alex Santo
Author photograph courtesy of Dion McIntosh

Library of Congress Cataloging-in-Publication Data
Names: McIntosh, Dion, author.
Title: Stop Being Invisible Companion Workbook. / Dion McIntosh
Description: First Edition. | Los Angeles : BadPeople, 2020.

Identifiers:
Subjects: LCSH: Entrepreneurship. | Success in business. | Influence (Psychology)
| BISAC: BUSINESS & ECONOMICS / Entrepreneurship. | BUSINESS & ECONOMICS /
E-Commerce / Internet Marketing. | SELF-HELP / Motivational & Inspirational.

Classification:

Version 09302020
Print ISBN: 978-1-7355830-2-0

A Message From the Author

Dion McIntosh

Congratulations on taking the first step to creating a human brand of greater influence.

The world of personal branding can be overwhelming, especially when you're just starting out. Take your time with this process. Be thorough, honest and detailed. Let it all out in these pages, the good, the bad and the ugly. This workbook is for your eyes only so don't shortchange yourself by cutting corners or trying to look good... keep it real. I assure you it will pay off in the end.

I can't wait to see what you do with your brand and the impact you'll make for so many others by clarifying and sharing your story. I'm deeply honored to play a part in helping you accomplish this. Please hit me up on social when you've completed your workbook and let me know your thoughts, questions or constructive criticisms. I'm always looking for ways to level up my work so your feedback is welcomed.

With humility and gratitude,

Dion McIntosh
Find me **@meetdion** on IG, FB & LI
Or my website: **www.dionmcintosh.com**

-INTRODUCTION-

Personal branding is about creating relatedness and connection with humans. When people hear how you got to where you are, the story behind it all, why you choose the business you're in, what matters to you most, what you hope for your customers or followers, what you stand for and who you are as a human being it brings people closer to you. It's attractive. Fans, followers, customers, team mates, investors, etc open up and listen to you differently when they can relate to you, when they believe you and when they like you. This is where influence happens. People who show themselves to the world in this way can move humans into action and truly make a profound impact. It's not about selling people your stuff. It's about connecting with people, sharing your truths, giving value and letting people see the human behind the art, product or service. From this place the right people will want to do business with you. Don't worry about that.

Equally as important you end up feeling more alive and inspired when you bring your full self to your work like this. Too many people don't bring their authentic selves to what they do and end up living uninspired, unfulfilling lives.

Your true self has been invisible long enough. No more hiding or pretending to be something you're not, it's exhausting. You're beautiful and perfect just as you are and the right people will love you, I promise.

Before we dive in and get to work on your brand I want to be certain you fully understand the power of getting this right.

"People unconsciously assume there is a parallel between one part and its whole."

Branding done right is both an art and a science. For now let's focus on the science. I'll try not to get too nerdy on you. All of us have a simultaneous unconscious and conscious mental filtering process that runs parallel when presented with data of any kind. This process sorts, categorizes and judges data (people, places and things) according to a number of filters. Some of those filters are designed to keep us from being eaten by dinosaurs and have been hardwired, and for good reason. While others were graciously donated to us by our parents, teachers, friends, environment, ex's etc. Some of these filters we are aware of and some we are not. This filtering process allows us to make conclusions or assumptions about a thing, person or situation almost instantly, whether it's true or not.

Big branding agencies know humans have this filtering process and intentionally architect messages to get you to think and feel what they intended, both consciously and on a deep unconscious level. They know that we've already been conditioned to believe certain things if presented in specific ways. They craft messages to compel us to think about their brand a certain way so we buy their products, use their service, visit their place of business or simply associate specific thoughts and feelings with their brand. Not everyone holds the same beliefs so they tailor these messages based on the type of person THEY want to speak to. It's why 100 people can watch the same commercial and some may cry, some may laugh, some may get angry and some won't even pay attention. The ones that cry may be the ones the brand is talking to and they have no interest in the other segments. That same brand could craft a new message and target a totally different group for the next campaign simply by reediting the commercial.

You have to think of your personal brand in the same manner. It doesn't matter what your business is, quite often people have to buy YOU first. If they don't like, trust or believe you, they will buy from someone else. If you didn't intentionally architect your brand with these considerations in mind then there's a good chance you're making people feel and think things about you and your business that you didn't intend.

In this workbook it is my intention to help you begin architecting an intentional human brand that connects with the right people, is true to you and clearly communicates who you are, what you do, why you do it and who you do it for. My goal is to help you become more inspired and connected to whatever work you do.

Self Awareness

"Your visions will become clear only when you can look into your own heart. Who looks outside, dreams; who looks inside, awakes."

— C.G. Jung

SECTION OVERVIEW

In this Self-Awareness section you'll be doing a lot of inner work. This is the most important part of your brand and it's the work most folks never fully do, if at all. It's why there are countless hollow human brands that come and go. You'll start to get clear on your why, strengths and weaknesses, values, passions, beliefs and goals by the end of this section. This will become the nucleus of your personal brand and will inform the crafting of your story, visuals and your entire brand ecosystem. If you do nothing else in this workbook your life and those around you will benefit from the work you do in this section.

"People can only connect with the version of yourself you're showing them. Let's ensure they're seeing the real you."

Passions:

- Visual beauty, music and gaming
- Startups and launching new ideas
- Helping people shed light on their internal shadows. Too many suffer in silence.
- Women empowerment. So many forces working against women to convince them they're not enough so they can be sold shit they don't need. My mom, wife and daughters deserve better.
- K-12 education (Current system is broken). Preparing our children for the future.
- Ending sex trafficking. Finding and supporting ways to solve this.

Vision: My vision is to help create a world where heart connected, transcendent business leaders who focus on people over profit becomes business as usual. Men and women who aren't afraid to share their truth, stand for what they believe in and bring who they truly are to everything they do. My mission is to be known as one of the ushers of this paradigm shift by helping these good men and women launch and refine their big ideas, build authentic personal brand platforms, teaching them how to overcome the inevitable dark times in business and showing them how to find a healthy equilibrium in their life. I believe this is my life purpose.

Being trusted with this mission is a great honor and privilege.

Section
02

Story Development

"To be a person is to have a story to tell."

– Isak Dinesen

Story Development

As you go through the stages below try to remember how you were thinking and feeling during each phase of life. Share what you learned from each of the moments. What did you take from those experiences? What lessons can you share with others? Don't hold back. Don't filter your answers, just dump as much information as you can as this will get distilled down to a clear brand story when you're done with the workbook. It's surprising to me, when I brand some of our clients, and they start telling me their story they gloss over things that I end up having to go, "Whoa, whoa, whoa, tell me more about that," and I come to find out it's a huge monumental piece of what made up who they are. It was a huge turning point or a huge character development point that they overlook. A lot of people do it. So don't edit yourself; write it all down.

Part I:
Upbringing

Write down how you grew up, a little bit about your family dynamic, what area you grew up in, if you did any moving around and traveling, what were the major milestones that you can remember, whether they were positive or negative. Even if it's a pain you don't want to talk about, write it down. No one will see this, but you and all of it matters. All of that makes up who you are. It's important that you add that to your story because it's the real stuff.

_____

_____

_____

_____

_____

_____

_____

_____

Remember: Your life and story define who you are. And that's what's attractive to others.

Notes

_____

_____

_____

_____

_____

_____

_____

_____

_____

_____

_____

Part II

School & Education

What was school life like for you; from elementary to high school, all the way through college, if you went? How did you grow up? Was there bullying involved? Were you a bully? Did you enjoy school? Did you have a love of learning?

Whatever it is, write it down, talk about the milestones, the big, major events that you remember. Even if you think it was uneventful, write it down.

Remember: Authenticity is critical. People smell inauthenticity.

Notes

_____

_____

_____

_____

_____

_____

_____

_____

_____

_____

_____

Part III

Career & Hustle

Let's talk business. What moves did you make? What were your experiences in the "real world"? Write down all the juicy details of your past hustle all the way up until today. Did you immediately go into looking for jobs? Did you start your first business? What did you try? Did you get fired? Did you fall on your face your first go-around at being an entrepreneur?

_____

_____

_____

_____

_____

_____

_____

_____

Remember: Authenticity is critical. People smell inauthenticity.

Notes

_____

_____

_____

_____

_____

_____

_____

_____

_____

_____

_____

Part IV

Relationships

Your personal life and relationships matter. Family, friends, significant others? Define and describe your significant relationships in the past and today. Who's in your circle of influence? Have you been married or divorced? How's your relationship with your parents or whoever raised you? What about your close friends. Talk about your relationships throughout your life.

Then we're going to go back later and pick out the things that are really most optimal for your brand position. It'll all tie together; you don't have to worry about or stress about how it's going to fit together. Just have a little faith in the process.

_____

_____

_____

_____

_____

_____

_____

_____

Remember: People don't relate to perfection. Our losses and struggles are what built you today. Don't be afraid to share your faults, challenges, or downfalls. The more human you make yourself out to be, the more people others will connect with you.

Notes

_____

_____

_____

_____

_____

_____

_____

_____

_____

_____

_____

Expert Positioning

"I fear not the man who has practiced 10,000 kicks once, but I fear the man who has practiced one kick 10,000 times."

— Bruce Lee

Expert Positioning

Your expert positioning ties everything together for your audience so they can understand who you are - quickly and clearly. Your expert positioning is made of three components.

1. **Value Proposition & How You Help**
2. **Audience**
3. **Method of Delivery**

1. Value Proposition

The first piece of your expert positioning is your value proposition. To put it simply, your value proposition should say, "This is what I'm good at, what I do for others and how it will benefit you."

VALUE PROPOSITION EXAMPLE

I help executives, business owners and entrepreneurs tell their story to the world by architecting beautiful, authentic personal brand platforms so they can not only bring who they are to what they do, but attract their best customers, fans and teammates.

How I help:

1. **The ability to help anyone turn their big ideas into a real business.**
2. **Improve the sales process, marketing strategy and business model of any existing business.**
3. **Unearth and architect authentic, heart connected brand strategies, messaging and overall brand ecosystems for people and companies.**

What's your value proposition?

_____

_____

_____

_____

_____

Website

"Getting a quality website is not an expense but rather an investment."

— Dr. Christopher Dayagdag

Your Website

Your website will always be relevant and is the only asset you'll have on the Internet that is completely controlled by you. Other social channels and platforms change constantly over time - in relevance and popularity. Some platforms may decide they no longer like your content and may block you or change something that breaks your brand or causes you to lose important data. It's unpredictable and someone investing in their personal brand must have a safe place to tell their story.

QUICK TIPS FOR AN EFFECTIVE WEBSITE

Tell them what to do: Getting your audience onto your site is the first step. Once they arrive you have to ensure they get a clear, easy user experience (my personal taste is to also make it visually beautiful). Tell them what to do and make the flow simple and intuitive. Your call to action should be clear (i.e. fill out a form, call a number, buy something, download something, etc). Confused visitors will go away.

Above the fold: Everything a site visitor sees when first landing on your website without having to take any action is above the fold. This is the most important part of your site. It's the first impression and first opportunity to hook the audience. Treat this area as prime real estate.

Headline: Who are you and what's in it for the visitor? A headline is a very concise value proposition often located "above the fold". The headline should let them know they are in the right place if they are looking for someone like you. Once that is established, they'll continue on wherever you direct them to go.

> **Examples:**
> **"I teach people how to cook healthy meals from home."**
> **"I help authors publish their first book."**

Mobile First: Design your site with mobile in mind, first! Most users come from mobile phones and will immediately go away if your site doesn't look right or function properly on a mobile device.

How do you want users to experience your website? What do you want them to take away? What do you want them to do? This is your chance to communicate whatever you desire to the world. Make it count.

Make a list of sites you love so you can easily show a web designer your vision for your site. Make a list of items you still need in order for a designer to build or refresh your site (New photos, copy, product links, logo, videos etc)

Notes

_____

_____

_____

_____

_____

_____

_____

_____

Social Channels

"When you lose followers because of where you stand – you strengthen your tribe."

— Glen Gilmore

SOCIAL CHANNELS

so·cial me·di·a

/ˌsōSHəl ˈmēdēə/

noun

1. Websites and applications that enable users to create and share content or to participate in social networking.

Most people make the mistake of thinking social media is for selling their stuff to people, but that thinking is why most never scale. Don't get me wrong there are tactful ways to offer what you're selling and monetize social without actually pitching all the time. When's the last time you went on Facebook, Instagram or LinkedIn, for example, thinking to yourself "I can't wait to see what people will sell me today!" I'd venture to say never. Social media is about finding your tribe and making connections by sharing meaningful, entertaining, engaging content that provides value to others and shows your unique perspective on topics you care about. Transacting becomes so much easier once people know, like and trust you as an expert resource for useful content in your industry.

How To Find Your Audience And Content Style In 60 Days Or Less.

- **Create business pages on Facebook, Instagram and Youtube**
- **Start by creating 15, 2- 5 minute, value based video posts**
- **Topics should be interesting stories from your life and business**
- **Include an outcome and a lesson learned at the end of each video**
- **Be sure each video is based on your Expert Positioning, Passions and Beliefs**
- **Choose stories that can easily bridge into your core business.**
- **Pay to boost these videos instead of waiting for the algorithm to send you organic traffic**
- **Pay close attention to engagement, view length, shares etc. These are your winners.**
- **Create more content similar to the winners. Rinse and repeat.**

Dion's Example: "My personal brand got me kicked off the Mickey Mouse Club." I tell a story about how my lack of focus created a reputation with the producers that caused them to cut me from the show. I share how this made me see that how people experience me IS my brand and I started being very aware of how I come off. I worked on my brand and 4 years later I got signed to Disney's Hollywood Records. This topic can easily transition into the power of intentional branding, my book and other services I sell when the time is right.

YOUR 15 TOPICS

- Use an interesting, funny or weird headline on the top to grab people's attention
- Write your headline then write down a few talking points that help you tell each story
- Have fun. Be yourself. Share your truth. The right people will love you.

1. _____

2. _____

3. _____

4. _____

5. _____

6. _____

7. _____

8. _____

9. _____

10. _____

11. _____

12. _____

13. _____

14. _____

15. _____

Section
06
Personal Style

"Style is a way to say who you are without having to speak."

— Rachel Zoe

Personal Style

The way you dress and present yourself is critical. Your style is part of your brand ecosystem and your clothing should align with your overall expert positioning. How do you want people to view you when you walk in a room? Your clothes have a lot to say.

A new personal style can give you so much confidence and can make you feel incredible!
If you're a serious professional looking to level up your brand I recommend working with a professional stylist to put together an updated look. This section will help you more easily communicate your preferences.

1. **Which celebrity best resembles a personal fashion style you'd love for yourself?**
    Tip: Create a Pinterest board with photos from people wearing outfits or rockin hairstyles you'd love for yourself.

2. **List at least 5 words you want to communicate with your personal style?** (Class, intelligence, fun, relatable, wealth, etc)

3. **Let's say you just walked in to a business event and no one knows you. What do you want people to think about you before you even open your mouth?** (Obviously energy, body language, swag or lack thereof all play a part, but this section is about visual style.)

4. **What would you ideally like for your clothes to say about you both while working and in your personal life?** (These two answers might be very different)

5. **What types of clothes, fabrics, colors would you NEVER wear?**

_____

_____

_____

_____

_____

Notes

Photos & Videos

"There are no bad pictures; that's just how your face looks sometimes."

— Abraham Lincoln

Photos & Videos

Photo Tips:

- Hire someone who specializes in shooting humans
- Invest the money to get a handful of pillar photos you can use as your core brand shots
- Make sure you hire someone you're comfortable with who can capture your personality
- Photos that look like some cookie cutter, generic studio headshot are a waste of cash
- Check their portfolio to be sure they've done what you're looking for
- Shoot on multiple backgrounds in studio & outside environments to match your brand
- Get at least 3 looks (outfits) so you have a variety of options to play with
- Ask for retouching to make the photos pop if needed
- Make sure you get written approval to use your photos how you see fit
- Have someone on set who can touch up your hair, clothes and/or makeup
- Share your brand notes from this workbook to help your photographer "get" you

Photo Tips:

- Check yourself. Hair, clothing, shine, teeth
- Check your background. Make sure it's on brand
- Check your lighting. Buy a basic ring light
- Check your tone, posture, body language and attitude
- Be mindful of what you're saying in your videos
- Make sure everything is consistent with how you want to be seen.
- Watch your time and make sure that you are being clear and concise.
- If you're bored watching your videos everyone else will be. Have fun. Be excited
- Share your video with someone you trust and get their feedback
- Your first few videos aren't going to be great unless you've been trained.
- Keep improving and you'll become more comfortable.
- Use a tripod unless the content is suppose to be a handheld vibe
- Selfie style is good. No heavy production is necessary. Left to right phone angle is best
- Audio is critical. If you can get a wireless lapel mic that syncs to your phone get one
- Light your lovely face. Poorly lit videos don't perform as well

Notes

Copy

"What matters isn't storytelling. What matters is telling a true story well."

— Ann Handley

Copy

We're not all talented writers, but you can't let that hold you back from sharing your value. Don't let copywriting scare you.

Hire an editor to check your articles and posts. Fiverr is a cost-effective platform that allows you to hire an outsourcer for a very reasonable price. Give it a try. It's a lot easier than you think once you get going.

The other option, if you don't want to hire an editor is to own it and put it all out there anyway. As long as what you're saying provides value, not many people are going to care if there's a grammar mistake. Would you hold it against someone if you loved the content?

Remember: Write how you speak. Just be you. Always stay authentic and don't try to be anyone but yourself.

Have you ever read something that was so powerful, typos didn't matter? Sure you have. If your content is quality and your intent is pure, your audience won't turn against you.

Remember: The key is getting started.

In general, each piece you write is meant to lead to the next. So you want to leave your audience with a pleasant experience with every post, paragraph, or interaction with your written brand.

Hook them and hold their hand through the entire piece.

Pretend you are writing to a 10 year old with a very short attention span. You need to guide them where to go or they'll lose focus. Snap your fingers if you need to! Keep them interested and don't be afraid to push them along.

You should be aware of your words and choose words that cause the right impression, though. If aren't able to objectively see the tone of your writing, ask someone for a second opinion. Get feedback that will help you get better. People love providing feedback.

Notes

Design

"Good design is like a refrigerator—when it works, no one notices, but when it doesn't, it sure stinks."

— Irene Au

Design

You want your brand assets to be designed so they are welcoming and attractive. Sadly, most people rely on their preference, which often leads to disaster. But that just means you'll stand out that much more if you have a professional to help you out. Trust the experts.

Remember: You'll stand apart much more with the help of a design professional.

Let me give you some basics that you can be aware of when you're designing your assets. There are some basics for aesthetics that should be considered.

Be aware of the symmetry of things. Look at the balance of things. People are thrown off when things are off symmetrically.

Keep Design Simple

Simplify. Use the simplest of elements and allow a lot of white space so the audience can breath and aren't overwhelmed. The more complicated you get, the more cluttered you get, and the more it distracts your audience.

Logo Tips

Your logo shouldn't be a distraction, it should be simple and powerful. Your brand is about you and how you make people feel. You don't want to distract from that with a crazy logo. Remember, a logo is just another asset - another extension of you and your brand.

Draw your focus on a certain element of your logo such as the golden arches of McDonald's or Oprah's handwritten style logo. What do you want them to focus on and why? Choose one element to concentrate on.

Remember: Don't complicate or over think it.

Logo Design Basics Sheet

Simplify.

Simple logos almost always outperform complicated ones (of course, there are exceptions - Starbucks). People remember them easily. Plain and simple, human brand logos should be simple.

Examples: Nike, Apple, Adidas, Sony

Choose a relevant color scheme.

Trust the design professional you're working with. Just because your favorite color is green, doesn't mean your logo should be green. Choose according to your target audience preference and market research. If you have a good design team, they may already have a good sense.

Create something new.

Sure, you should observe logos, so you have an understanding of the psychology behind them, but don't do a classless copycat logo of something that already exists.

Get symmetrical.

Humans love symmetry. Make sure things are lined up and nothing is off-balance. Nothing can repel customers quicker than an imbalance that has no purpose. It screams "unprofessional".

Have meaning.

Humans like looking for clues. Each element of your logo provokes a feeling from your audience. Each design element should have a purpose and point to you as a person and a brand. There's no reason to have a random element in your logo.

It is a fantastic idea to make some clever logos, which can help you to tell your story.

State your name.

For the most part, you will probably want your entire name to appear with your logo mark, at least have a version that includes it.

Be you. On brand.

Most importantly, the logo should speak to you and about you. If you're having a designer build your logo, you should look at the final product and say, "That's me right there". After all, it is now a big part of you and your brand. It may even be seen more than you are yourself.

Outsourcing

"If you really want to grow as an entrepreneur, you've got to learn to delegate."

— Richard Branson

Outsourcing

Revisit your strengths and weaknesses and identify which things are dragging you down. These are the tasks you are going to want to pass off to an outsourcer. But first you must understand how to outsource and manage expectations.

Outsourcing Tips:
1. Be clear on your objective. What EXACTLY do you want from the outsourcer?
2. Beware of language and interpretation barriers.
3. Ask clarifying questions. Make them repeat all instructions back to you.
4. Look at their portfolio!
5. Look for a team who has executed to your standards.
6. Make sure communication works in the beginning. Or run.

Remember: Relationships end how they begin.

Outsourcing Checklist and Resources

Here are a few questions you might want to ask while vetting the team that handles your brand.

- ☐ Have you built successful brands for entrepreneurs in a similar position to where I am at currently
- ☐ What have your previous clients experienced as a result of your branding efforts?
- ☐ What is your process for building brands specifically for individuals and entrepreneurs?
- ☐ How do you decide what color scheme to use for individuals?
- ☐ How many people will be working on my brand at any given time?
- ☐ Who is on your team and how are they an expert in their respective discipline?

When looking at their portfolio, ask yourself these questions.

- ☐ Has this team produced the types of content you want created?
- ☐ Is their work flawless in design and logic?
- ☐ Do they create easy-to-use user experiences for their clients' audiences?
- ☐ Is their work compelling and engaging?
- ☐ Does it pull the reader in and demand attention?

Popular Resources For Design Outsourcing
Fiverr.com
99designs.com
Upwork.com

Notes

Notes

Notes

Section
Our Work

Client Showcase

A Mother Loses Her Son

To Tragedy And Starts Helping Others Cope With Loss.

Wanda Shelton's story is both heartbreaking and inspirational. She developed ways to overcome grief through her own personal tragedy, but her message was being hidden under outdated visuals and large blocks of heavy text that people just don't read in today's fast paced world. Wanda's story covers some heavy subject matter, but when positioned in a modern, clear brand more people can now hear her message.

Before

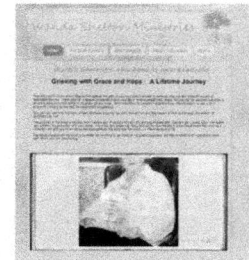
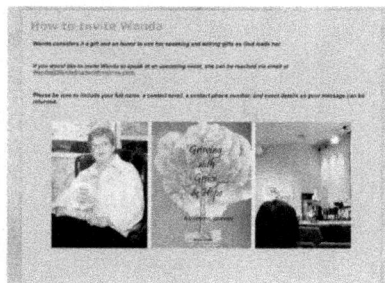

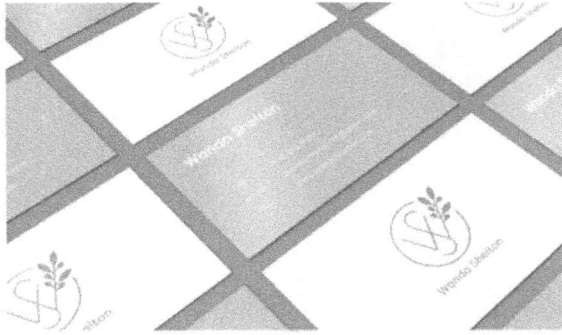

Wanda Shelton

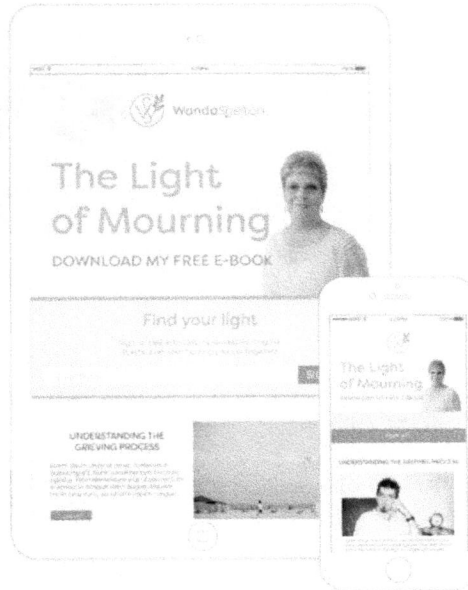

Dr. Terence Young

Doctor Who Delivered 1000's of Babies Turns Digital Entrepreneur

Dr. Terence Young's walked away from his 20 year medical career to start an online business. He's smart, methodical and hard working, but his online profile was so fragmented and confusing it virtually attracted no one.
Terence now has the personal brand of a power player. He has a book hitting Amazon soon, his own product line in the works and a rock solid brand platform.

After

TERENCE
YOUNG

	#6BC7C0
	#4DA1B0
	#266682
	#13334D
	#051A37

Typeface:
Futura

Style:
Medium

Business Card

Social Media

Product

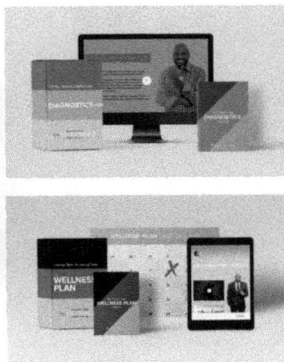

Podcast

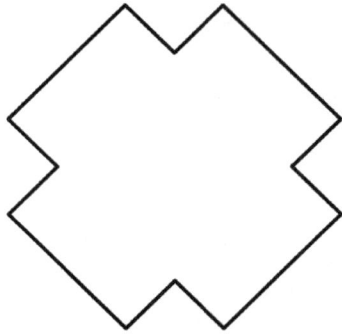

DO IT
YOURSELF
BRANDING

LEARN MORE AT:

WWW.**STOPBEINGINVISIBLEBOOK**.COM

WWW.**DOITYOURSELFBRANDING**.COM

WWW.**DIONMCINTOSH**.COM